So Far from Home

T0363464

Written by Nancy O'Connor

Illustrated by Lyn Stone

Flying Start
to Literacy®

Contents

Chapter 1

Flew away

20 May, In the mountains

Angie watched Dad remove Lucy's leather hood. The falcon's sharp talons gripped Dad's leather glove. She made a soft *scree-scree* call – as if in anticipation of what she knew was coming. The hunt!

Angie's dad was a master falconer. He had learnt the sport of hunting with birds of prey from his father, and now he was teaching it to her. For Angie, nothing was more exciting than watching a hawk or falcon soar into the sky. Other kids might go fishing with their fathers, but she loved falconry!

"Do you really think Lucy's ready, Dad?" Angie asked. A frown wrinkled her forehead. "I'm worried that we haven't trained her long enough."

"Well, we're going to give her a chance to show us what she can do," said Dad.

Lucy was their new falcon, and Angie thought she was the most beautiful raptor they'd ever had. This was the first time they had taken Lucy into the mountains by the river. After training her in their large backyard for the past month, she now flew obediently from her perch to both of them, and was always rewarded with bits of meat. The day had come to see what she would do in the wild.

"Can you check the tracking device?" asked Dad.

Angie looked at the transmitter on Lucy's leg. She reached into her pocket, took out the tracking device and turned it on.

"It's working perfectly," she said.

"Okay, Lucy. There you go!" Dad raised his arm and cast off the bird. She stretched her wings and flew up towards the sky.

"Help me flush out some prey," said Dad.

Angie began walking through the tall grass, making sweeping movements with her arms and feet. She hoped the motion would startle some small animal from its hiding place. Dad did the same thing on the far side of the clearing. Lucy watched from her perch.

A rabbit burst from the grass right in front of Angie.

"Here, Dad!" she called out as the animal raced away. They watched as Lucy lifted off her branch. She dove towards the ground and struck the leaping rabbit midair. She used her sharp beak to kill it, then came to rest in the grass.

"We'll need to allow her to eat some of her kill," Dad told Angie, "the way she would if she lived in the wild. But we can't let her hoard it."

He approached the falcon slowly and offered a tidbit of meat to her, coaxing Lucy back onto his gloved hand. "Good job, girl," Dad said to the falcon. "That was exactly what we trained you to do."

"I'll bag the rabbit, Dad," Angie said. It would be a meal for Lucy when they got her back to the cage in their backyard.

"Great. Let's try it again," said Dad.

This time, Lucy flew much higher. She circled the meadow three times. Angie could faintly hear the bird's bells as Lucy flew overhead, searching for prey.

"Should we start flushing, Dad?" she asked.

"Yep, let's go." They started across the meadow, talking loudly and shuffling their feet through the grass.

Suddenly, an angry cry cut through the air. Angie and her dad looked up just as a red-tailed hawk swooped down towards the falcon. It struck at her with strong talons, then veered away. Lucy tumbled towards the ground.

"Dad!" Angie screamed. "She's being attacked!"

Lucy recovered, flapped her powerful wings and soared high once more. The large hawk was in close pursuit, but the falcon's superior speed quickly put distance between them. Lucy sped out over the river. She soon became just a speck in the sky. The pursuing hawk became a second speck.

"Where's she going?" Angie cried. "Will the hawk kill her?"

"She'll get away from him," said Dad. "Remember, she's the fastest animal on Earth. Get the tracking device."

Angie pulled it out. A dotted path moved east up the river, into the wilderness. They watched the screen until it stopped beeping.

"Out of range," Angie whispered, and wiped a tear from her cheek with the sleeve of her jacket. Dad put his arm around her and they waited. And waited.

Chapter 2

Stolen

5 June, Tyler's place

"I'm going out to feed the chickens, Mum!" Tyler called.

"Good. I'm glad I didn't have to remind you again." She grinned at him. "And get –"

"Eggs," Tyler said. "I know."

Tyler's mum thought eating organic eggs made everyone healthier. It was his job to let the chickens out of the coop and feed them every morning before he left for school.

"Come on, Sally," Tyler said to his favourite hen. "Get moving." She was always the last one to get off her nest and leave the coop. When Tyler scattered chicken feed across the ground, Sally ran to eat with the others. He began searching the nests for eggs and soon found four.

Suddenly, there was a loud ruckus out in the yard. Tyler jerked to a stand and slammed the back of his head against the top of the coop. "Ouch!" he cried.

When he turned around, he saw a red-tailed hawk gripping Sally in its talons. The other chickens were running in circles around the pen, flapping and squawking.

"No!" Tyler yelled. "Let go of her!" He rushed towards the hawk, which stared at him with its beady dark eyes, then flapped its broad wings and lifted Sally into the morning sky.

"Mum!" he shouted.

His mother rushed out of the house. "What's wrong?"
She looked up and clapped her hand over her mouth.
Sally was gone.

When Tyler got on the bus a few minutes later, his friend
Scott greeted him. "Hey, man, what's going on? You look
like your best friend just died."

"Sally got carried off by a hawk this morning."

Scott's eyes grew round. "Who's Sally?"

"One of our chickens," Tyler replied. "I know you're
thinking it's just a stupid chicken, but I liked her the best."

"That's awful!" his friend said. "Did you see it happen?"

"Yeah, I had just let the chickens out into the yard and was collecting eggs when I heard all this noise. The hawk swooped down and grabbed Sally in its claws. It was terrible! *I hate* hawks! I'd like to kill all of them!"

"I don't blame you," Scott said.

"Mum said the hawk was just doing what hawks do," Tyler said. "Hunting. Like that's supposed to make me feel any better."

The bus pulled up in front of Mission Primary School, and the boys grabbed their backpacks and stood to get off.

13

Chapter 3

Rescued

9 September, At the canyon

Tyler and Scott had decided to go riding in the canyon after school. Skidding their tyres and kicking up dust, they came to a stop right next to the railroad fence. They wiped the sweat and dust off their faces with their T-shirts.

"We should have brought some water," Scott said. "I'm dying of thirst."

"Me, too," Tyler gasped. "I wish –" He pointed. "What's that?"

Near the fence, something was flapping around and making terrible screeching sounds. The boys dropped their bikes and approached cautiously. The creature began to thrash from side to side. Its shrill cries were earsplitting.

"It's a bird," Scott exclaimed. "Maybe a hawk. One of its wings is tangled in the fence wire." He looked at Tyler. "We should rescue it."

"No way!" his friend said. "This is my chance to get even for Sally."

"Don't be stupid!" Scott shouted. "That's not the bird that took your chicken, and anyway, it's injured!"

"I guess you're right," Tyler grumbled. "Hey, look. There are bells tied to its feet. What the heck?"

The boys moved closer.

"It must belong to someone," Scott said. "Let's get help."

The boys grabbed their bikes and pushed them up the hill as fast as they could. When they reached the road, they sped to Tyler's house.

Tyler's mum looked up the number for Animal Control, and the boys called to report the injured bird. Then they raced back to the canyon to wait for the officers. When the truck pulled up, two people in uniform climbed out.

"I'm Officer Torres," the woman said. "And this is Officer King. But you can just call us Sylvia and Mike. Where exactly did you see the raptor?"

"Raptor?" Scott said, his eyes growing wide. "I thought raptors were dinosaurs!"

Mike laughed. "Those raptors lived a long time ago. *Raptor* is another name for a bird of prey, like hawks and owls. They hunt and catch small animals, instead of eating seeds or worms like songbirds do. Let's get going."

Sylvia opened the back of the truck and took out a cardboard box. Mike picked up a pair of heavy gloves and a towel, and the boys led the way down the hillside.

"You were smart to call us," Sylvia said. "Raptors have sharp beaks and strong talons."

"Yeah, I know all about that," Tyler grumbled. "A hawk carried off one of my chickens during the summer. I hate them!"

"I hear you," Mike said, "but it's just instinct – like migration."

The moment the bird saw the group approaching, it began shrieking and struggling. Mike put his gloves on and picked up the towel.

"Stand back," he ordered. "We don't want it to hurt itself any further."

"You're right, boys," Sylvia observed. "It has bells on its legs – and jesses. It belongs to someone."

Mike crept forward and draped the towel gently over the bird. The bird immediately stopped moving. Holding it carefully, Mike nodded to his partner. "Okay, you can cut the wire now."

Sylvia snipped several spots on the fence where the bird's wing was entangled. Mike lifted up the wrapped bird to show the boys. Sylvia opened the lid of the box, and Mike put the bird inside. When the lid was nearly closed, he slowly pulled out the towel.

"That does it! Now we need to get this little falcon to the Raptor Rescue Centre."

"I thought it was a hawk," Tyler said as the group hiked
back up the hill. "And what are jesses?"

Mike turned back to him. "It's actually a female peregrine
falcon. They're usually darker in colour than hawks.
Somebody has trained it to hunt. Jesses are the leather
straps hunters put around their bird's legs. They're fastened
to a leash, so the bird can be controlled."

"Birds can be used for hunting?" Scott asked. "I never knew that. What sort of animals do they hunt?"

"Mostly small creatures, like rabbits and mice," Mike said.

"And chickens," Tyler said.

"A hunter would never train a falcon to steal people's chickens. You boys should go home and do an Internet search on falconry. It's an ancient sport."

"Cool," Scott said. "Where's the Raptor Rescue Centre?"

"Up in the foothills," said Sylvia. "There's a woman there who takes in injured and orphaned birds of prey."

"Could we call her tomorrow to see how the bird is doing?" Tyler asked. When Scott threw him a quizzical look, Tyler grinned and shrugged. "Well, we saved her life. Don't you think we should check on her?"

"Her name is Caroline Graham," said Sylvia as she handed Tyler a business card. "Thanks again, boys, for calling us. A lot of people think it's okay to take home an animal they find in the wild. They want to turn it into a pet, but that's against the law."

"Why?" asked Tyler.

"The Department of Fish and Wildlife has lots of regulations for protecting our wildlife," Mike said. "Give Mrs Graham a call and she can tell you more about it." He put the box containing the bird in the back of the truck. "Don't worry. She'll take good care of this girl."

Chapter 4

Reunited

10 September, Raptor Rescue Centre

Caroline Graham answered her telephone on Saturday afternoon with a cheerful, "Raptor Rescue!"

Scott hesitated. "I'm Scott Meyer, one of the boys who found a falcon yesterday, and . . . and we want to know if it's okay."

"Oh, thanks for calling to check on her. She's doing just fine. She was a little underweight, so I gave her a nice fat rat for dinner last night."

Scott grimaced. "Um . . . is there any chance we could come to your rescue centre and see her?"

"Sure, as long as an adult brings you. But you better hurry because I think she'll be going home soon."

"*Home?* How do you know where she lives?" Scott asked.

"I'll explain when you get here," Caroline said.

"We're on our way!" When Scott hung up the phone he and Tyler high-fived each other and went to find Scott's dad.

The boys were disappointed to see that the Raptor Rescue Centre looked like a regular house. They had expected something more like a zoo or farm. Caroline met them at the front door and invited them to follow her around the house and through a side gate, to the backyard.

A large aviary filled much of the yard. She opened the door and invited them in. Inside, there were many smaller cages, and in those cages were more than a dozen birds.

"Now, let's take a look at the falcon. I'll bet she has a story to tell."

The bird was in a cage by herself.

"Fortunately, her wing is just bruised," Caroline said. "She's worn out and a little underweight, so she had a good dinner last night."

"A rat, right?" Mr Meyer grinned. "The boys told me all about it on the way up here."

"In the wild, raptors catch mice and other rodents. So I give them a rat every day while they're in my care. I buy the rats frozen, by the dozen. They cost about four dollars a piece. That adds up when I have eight or ten birds I'm rehabbing."

"Wow, that's like $280 a week!" Tyler exclaimed.

"But sometimes I can save money by picking up roadkill."

"Ewww!" Scott exclaimed. "Gross!"

"I pick up dead animals that have been recently hit by cars. They have to be very fresh, though, or they could make the birds sick."

Caroline's phone rang. "I'll be back in a minute." She stepped out of the enclosure and crossed the yard.

When she returned, three people were with her – a man, a woman and a girl who looked about ten.

"Meet the Herreras," Caroline said. "This is John and Clara and their daughter, Angie." Then she gestured at the boys. "These are the young men who found your falcon. And this is Scott's father, Mr Meyer." Everyone shook hands.

"The Herreras have driven all the way down here from the mountains because they love this bird so much," Caroline said.

Angie eagerly asked, "Can I see her?"

"Come on, we'll show you where she is," Tyler said. He led the group back to the falcon's cage.

"That's my Lucy!" Angie cried as she stepped into the cage alone. She whistled to Lucy and called her name. The falcon stared at her and gave a soft cry. "Mum, Dad, she remembers me! After all this time."

"She's your bird?" Tyler asked, surprised.

"She belongs to my dad, but I helped train her," Angie explained.

"When Animal Control brought her to me yesterday," Caroline said, "I called the Fish and Wildlife office and gave them the number from the band on Lucy's leg." She laughed. "The guy on the phone argued with me, saying I had to be mistaken. He said the bird with that number belonged to some people who live a thousand kilometres away. But he finally gave me their phone number, so I called them."

"And here we are!" said Mr Herrera. "We drove eighteen hours, almost nonstop. Angie barely let us take breaks. We lost Lucy over three months ago and gave up hope of ever seeing her again."

"I never gave up hope." A smile stretched across Angie's face as she stroked the barred feathers on Lucy's chest.

"How did you lose her?" Scott asked.

Angie's dad explained. "Angie, Lucy and I were in the mountains hunting last May. It was Lucy's first day out and a hawk attacked her. It must have frightened her badly."

"We waited and waited for her to come back," Angie chimed in, "but she didn't."

Mr Herrera continued. "A falconer understands that each time you take a bird out, there's a chance it won't come back. Sometimes, their instincts take over and they just fly away. And Lucy's tracking device came off somehow."

Mrs Herrera laughed. "Lucy might have been lost forever if it wasn't for her accident here – and for you boys."

"She was so far from home," Angie said softly. "Thank you." She smiled at the boys.

"And this centre is a great rescue operation," Mr Herrera said. "There's something we want you to have." He handed a folded paper to Caroline. "Consider it our thank-you."

She gasped. It was a cheque for $500! "I hardly know what to say. I've been rescuing and caring for raptors for over 30 years because I love doing it. Thank you so much, but my real reward is when there's a happy ending like this one."

"Maybe now you won't need to pick up as much roadkill," Scott said, making everyone laugh.

The National Bank
Pay: Raptor Rescue
The sum of: Five hundred dollars

"We brought something for you boys, too," Mr Herrera said. He pulled two small leather hoods out of a bag and handed one to each of them. "When we take our falcons out, we always put hoods on them. It keeps them calm, and they won't try to fly until the hood is removed. Then they know it's time to hunt."

"Wow! It's beautiful," said Scott.

"Yeah, thank you," Tyler agreed.

"And this is Lucy's hood." Mr Herrera gave it to Angie. She slipped it over Lucy's head and tied it with two leather thongs. From the top of the hood sprouted a cluster of reddish feathers. Only her sharp yellow beak stuck out.

"Wow, she looks like a soldier," said Scott.

"She does, doesn't she?" Angie agreed.

"Well, it's time to get going," Mr Herrera said. "We've got another long drive ahead of us." He pulled a leather glove from the bag and slipped it on. Walking up to Lucy, he pressed his arm against her chest. She stepped right up on the glove and stood there, turning her hooded head from right to left and stretching her wings.

Angie smiled. "I think she knows she's going home."

A note from the author

I could not have written this story without the help of an old friend. Kandie Barnett Cansler is one of the leading raptor rehabilitation experts in Southern California, and has done this work for over 30 years.

When I interviewed her, she told me many stories about birds she has rescued. *So Far from Home* is based on one of those stories. Kandie is licensed by the California Department of Fish and Wildlife and does not get paid for her work. Caring for injured or orphaned birds takes a lot of time and is costly. Kandie also confirmed that roadkill is occasionally part of her birds' diets. She told me this gruesome fact while we were eating lunch!

Thank you, Kandie, for sharing your stories and answering all my questions. It's clear you are passionate about the work you do.